Taos
A Pictorial Guide for Travelers

TAOS

A PICTORIAL GUIDE FOR TRAVELERS

Michael Butler

SUNSTONE
PRESS

SANTA FE

All photographs by the author.

Sunstone books may be purchased for educational, business, or sales promotional use.
For information please write: Special Markets Department, Sunstone Press,
P.O. Box 2321, Santa Fe, New Mexico 87504-2321.

Book and cover design › R. Ahl
Printed on acid-free paper
∞

Library of Congress Cataloging-in-Publication Data

Names: Butler, Mike, 1950- author.
Title: Taos : a pictorial guide for travelers / by Michael Butler.
Description: Santa Fe, NM : Sunstone Press, 2019. | Includes bibliographical
  references and index.
Identifiers: LCCN 2019014421 | ISBN 9781632932648 (pbk. : alk. paper)
Subjects: LCSH: Taos (N.M.)--Guidebooks. | Taos (N.M.)--Pictorial works. |
  Taos (N.M.)--History.
Classification: LCC F804.T2 B883 2019 | DDC 917.89/5304--dc23
LC record available at https://lccn.loc.gov/2019014421

WWW.SUNSTONEPRESS.COM
SUNSTONE PRESS / POST OFFICE BOX 2321 / SANTA FE, NM 87504-2321 /USA
(505) 988-4418 / ORDERS ONLY (800) 243-5644 / FAX (505) 988-1025

Taos Morada and Taos Mountain

CONTENTS

8   Map of Taos

9   Introduction

12   Pueblo Peak (Taos Mountain)

14   Taos Pueblo

16   Rio Grande Del Norte National Monument

18   Rio Grande Gorge Bridge

20   Taos Ski Valley

22   La Hacienda De Los Martinez

24   St. Francis of Assisi Church

26   Taos Morada

28   Governor Bent House And Museum

30   Kit Carson Home And Museum

32   Long John Dunn House And Bridge

34   Historic Taos Inn

36   Taos Society of Artists: Ernest Blumenschein Home And Museum

38   Taos Society of Artists: Bert Geer Phillips Home And Studio

40   Taos Society of Artists: Couse/Sharp Historic Site

42   Taos Society of Artists: Victor Higgins Home and Studio

44   Mabel Dodge Luhan House

46   Nicolai Fechin House/Taos Art Museum

48   Historic Taos County Courthouse

50   Historic Courthouse Fresco Murals

52   Harwood Museum of Art

54   Millicent Rogers Museum

56   Taos First Presbyterian Church

58   Greater World Earthship Community

60   Bibliography

Taos & Vicinity

Map Numbers Refer to Page Numbers

Map Not to Scale

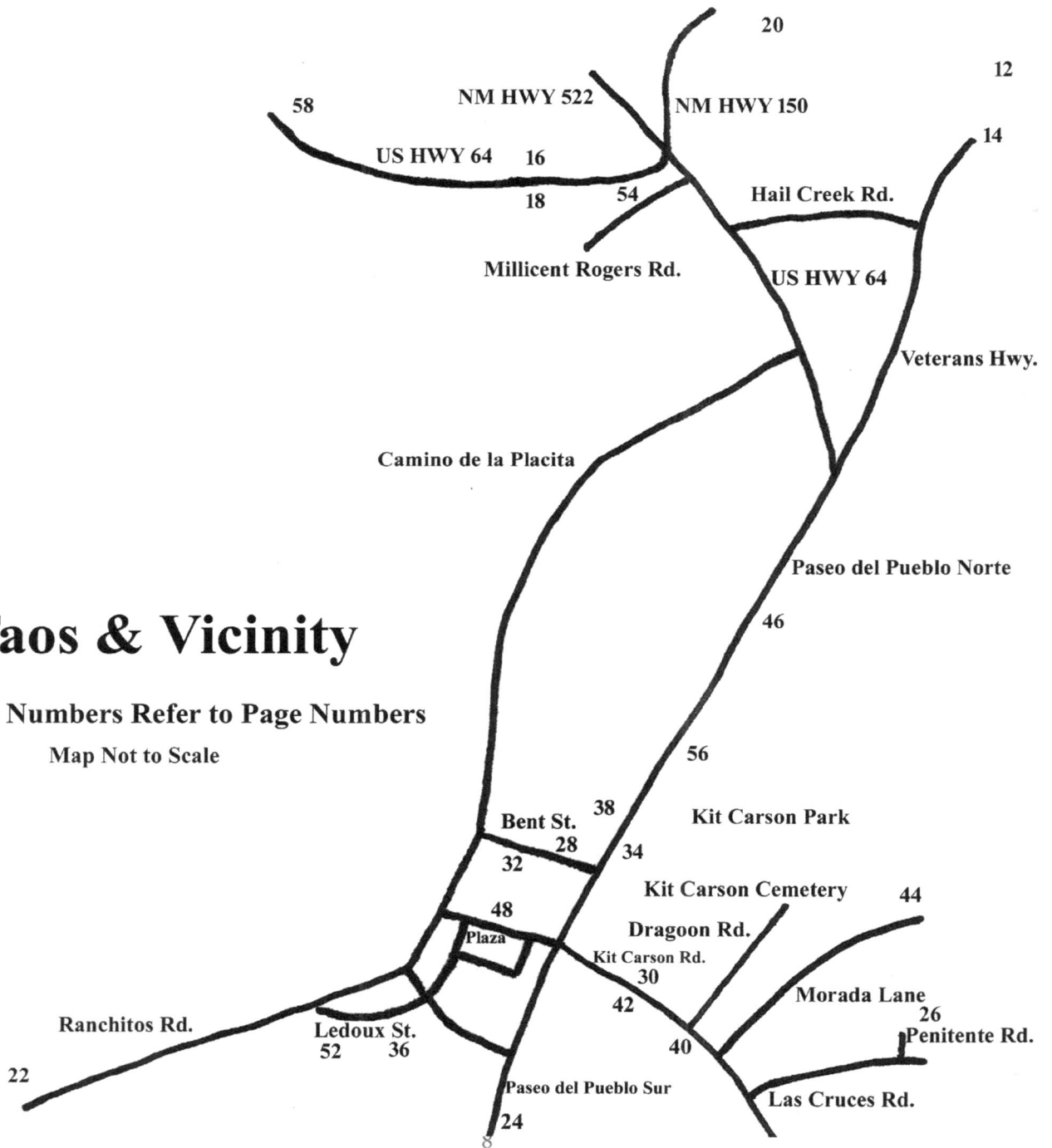

20

12

NM HWY 522

NM HWY 150

58

US HWY 64   16

14

18   54

Hail Creek Rd.

Millicent Rogers Rd.

US HWY 64

Veterans Hwy.

Camino de la Placita

Paseo del Pueblo Norte

46

56

Bent St.   38

28

Kit Carson Park

32   34

48

Kit Carson Cemetery

44

Plaza

Dragoon Rd.

Kit Carson Rd.

30

Morada Lane

26

Ranchitos Rd.

42

Penitente Rd.

Ledoux St.

40

52   36

22

Paseo del Pueblo Sur

Las Cruces Rd.

8   24

INTRODUCTION

Few travelers to Taos today realize that they are entering one of the oldest continuously occupied areas in the United States. Most realize that Taos Pueblo is "pretty old," but actually, settlement of the area pre-dates the Pueblo. At the Pot Creek archaeological site just a few miles south of Taos on New Mexico Highway 158, archaeologists discovered the remains of pit houses that dated back to about 1000 A.D. Further excavations of these "Ancestral Puebloan" sites revealed that the pit houses eventually gave way to one-story adobe homes, and then multi-story adobe homes. The multi-story structure at Pot Creek was probably abandoned about 1320, when it appears that it burned down. The inhabitants then moved on to create multi-story pueblos at Picuris and Taos. Archaeologists have dated the construction of Taos Pueblo at about 1350 A.D., and it still stands today.

European incursion into New Mexico began when the expedition of Francisco Vasquez de Coronado crossed the Rio Grande from Mexico and went northwest to Zuni Pueblo in 1540. The Spaniards were seeking the fabled "Seven Cities of Cibola" which were rumored to be wealthy with gold and silver. Coronado found no gold and silver there, so he sent an advance scouting party led by Hernando de Alvardo out to search further. Alvarado reached Taos Pueblo in the summer of 1540, but again, no gold or silver was found.

Disappointed, the Spaniards retreated to Mexico, and didn't venture back north until 1598 when Don Juan de Onate led an expedition north along the Rio Grande. After a six-month journey they reached a pueblo just north of what is today the town of Espanola. Onate named it San Juan Pueblo. Today it is known by its native name "Ohkay Owingeh." Onate established New Mexico's first capital at a site west of the Rio Grande, across from San Juan Pueblo. He named it San Gabriel. It was later replaced by Santa Fe as the capital in 1610. Onate continued his journey northward, reaching Picuris Pueblo on July 13, and Taos Pueblo on July 14, 1598.

Spanish rule of the pueblos was rather brutal. Beatings and forced labor were common, and the native religion was suppressed by the Catholic priests. By August of 1680 the pueblo people had had enough. The disparate pueblos of New Mexico were united as one by a charismatic leader from San Juan Pueblo named Po'Pay. Runners were sent to all the pueblos to let the people know the date when Po'Pay's rebellion would begin. The Spanish were caught off guard when the coordinated rebellion began, and they were thoroughly routed by the enraged pueblo people. Over 1,000 Spaniards were killed, including 70 in Taos, of which two were Franciscan priests. The Spaniards were forced to retreat from Taos Pueblo, San Juan Pueblo, all the pueblos along the Rio Grande, out of Santa Fe, and all the way south of the Rio Grande at El Paso back to Mexico.

The Spanish were vanquished from New Mexico for twelve years. The re-conquest began in 1692 when Don Diego de Vargas marched with troops north from Mexico, conquering one pueblo after another, freeing the town of Santa Fe, and marching all the way to Taos Pueblo. By 1696, the rebellion was over.

The Spanish government began asserting control over the area by awarding large land grants to loyal individuals and families. The purpose was to discourage further pueblo uprisings, and prevent incursion by French and American traders and trappers who had their eyes upon this area. In 1710 a land grant was awarded to Captain Cristobal de la Serna, who was rewarded for his service at Taos Pueblo. This area is just south of the town of Taos today. In 1796, the Don Fernando de Taos land grant was awarded. The land grants did not guarantee immediate occupation however. Raids on the fledgling Spanish communities by hostile tribes such as Comanche, Apache, and Ute prevented permanent settlement. The Ranchos de Taos area was settled by a few Spanish ranchers in the 1730s and by 1760 a small community had grown up. It had to be abandoned due to fierce Comanche raids from 1760 to 1779. The settlers were forced to take refuge in Taos Pueblo. They eventually returned about 1780, and from 1813–1815 built their famous Saint Francis of Assisi church in the town plaza.

In 1821, Mexico gained independence from Spain, and this opened the way for the Santa Fe Trail. Spain had fiercely restricted travel by Americans to Santa Fe, but the new independent government was unable to stop the lucrative trade with the Americans. In 1846 the United States went to war with Mexico. A U.S. army force led by Col. Stephen Watts Kearney invaded Santa Fe and captured it without a shot being fired. Certain groups in Taos received the news with horror. They did not want American government. On January 19, 1847 a group of Taos Pueblo Indians and Spanish settlers broke into the home of Charles Bent, the newly appointed American governor of the territory. Bent and several other Americans were killed in what became known as the Taos Revolt. When word of the revolt reached Santa Fe, Col. Sterling Price was sent north with a force of 335 U.S. soldiers to quell the rebellion. Finding most of the rebels holed up in the San Jeronimo church in Taos Pueblo, the army bombarded the church with cannon fire and destroyed it, killing most of the people inside. The rebellion was crushed. The war with Mexico ended with a U.S. victory in 1848, and the Treaty of Guadalupe-Hidalgo awarded the New Mexico Territory to the Americans. New Mexico became the 47th state in the Union in 1912.

Taos thus traces its roots to the construction of Taos Pueblo in 1350, and Spanish settlement in the early 1700s. Its history has not always been peaceful, and even today relations between natives, Hispanics, and Anglos can be tense at times. But over the years a multi-cultural dynamic has evolved from the cooperation of all the groups, and it makes Taos the special place that it is today.

December full moon rising over Taos Mountain

Pueblo Peak (Taos Mountain)

Rising to a height of 12,305 feet, Pueblo Peak towers over Taos Pueblo and the town of Taos to the south, and the Rio Grande Valley to the west. It rises abruptly from the high plains, part of an upthrust of the Sangre de Cristo mountains which occurred about 70 million years ago. Taos Pueblo Indians have always regarded the mountain and Blue Lake at its southeast base as sacred places. When Carson National Forest was created by the U.S. government on July 1, 1908, Blue Lake was included in the forest. Blue Lake became a popular destination for hikers and fishermen, much to the dismay of the Indians. The visitors left litter and degraded places along the lake shore, desecrating the ancient sacred place. The Pueblo began a 60 year battle for the return of Blue Lake, petitioning Congress and fighting in the courts. Their efforts were finally rewarded in 1970 when Blue Lake and the surrounding 48,000 acres were ceded to the Taos Pueblo Reservation.

New Mexico's highest peak, Wheeler Peak, cannot be seen from Taos because it sits behind Pueblo Peak. Five miles northeast of Pueblo Peak, Wheeler Peak's 13,161 foot summit can best be seen from the Moreno Valley near Angel Fire. Wheeler Peak is a popular hiking destination in summer, accessed on the west side by a trail starting from Twining (Taos Ski Valley). It is a steep ascent from Williams Lake which is in a cirque depression created by glaciers from the Pleistocene era about 15,000 years ago. The glaciers carved out U-shape valleys, and left behind piles of rocks known as moraines. At Williams Lake, moraines can be seen north and west of the lake. Williams Lake is named for famed mountain man "Old Bill" Williams.

Mining in the Sangre de Cristo mountains near Taos boomed in the 1880s, with the discovery of copper at Twining and gold at Red River. The deposits were not extensive though, and the mining boom only lasted until about 1920. The parking lot at Taos Ski Valley roughly occupies the area of what was once Twining. Molybdenum mining has provided jobs for hundreds of people in Questa since the mine opened in 1916 nine miles east of town. However, the mine was closed by its owner Chevron in 2014, and environmental rehabilitation of the area has begun.

TAOS PUEBLO
THREE MILES NORTH OF TAOS PLAZA

According to legend, Taos Pueblo was founded 1,000 years ago by a great chief who followed an eagle to the Rio Pueblo at the foot of Pueblo Peak. The eagle dropped two feathers- one on the north side of the river and one on the south side, so the great five-story adobe structures of Taos Pueblo were built on each side of the river. Whatever the original founding date, it is certain that the Spanish first viewed the pueblo in the summer of 1540 when Captain Hernando de Alvarado and his men arrived. Alvarado was leading an advance party for Francisco Vasquez de Coronado, who was exploring northern New Mexico searching for the Seven Cities of Cibola.

Taos Pueblo is built of adobe bricks, which must be re-plastered with mud almost every year to preserve the bricks. Originally there were no doors or windows on the ground floor to prevent intrusion by raiding tribes such as the Comanche and Apache. Entry was gained by ladders from the ground to a hole in the roof. The ladders could be pulled up in case of attack. By about 1830, the hostile raids diminished and a strong trade flourished between Taos Pueblo, Plains Indian tribes, and the mountain men.

Entering Taos Pueblo today, visitors first see the ruins of a church to the north, and a beautiful adobe church on the south which is the mission church of San Geronimo de Taos completed in 1850. The original Spanish mission church was built in 1619. This church was destroyed by the U.S. Army in January, 1847 as a result of resistance by certain Taos Indians and Hispanic residents of Taos who objected to the U.S. occupation of this Mexican territory. The Army believed that perpetrators of the resistance sought shelter in the Taos Pueblo church, so the church was bombarded and destroyed, along with many innocent people inside. The grounds of the ruined church serve as the Taos Pueblo cemetery today.

About 1,800 people live on the Taos Pueblo Reservation today. In 2015 it was reported that no one lives in the ancient Pueblo dwellings anymore, due to their lack of electricity and running water. Taos Pueblo Reservation contains about 105,000 acres, so residents live in modern dispersed homes and participate in traditional farming and ranching livelihoods. Taos Pueblo welcomes visitors throughout the year except from February to April when it is closed to the public.

Rio Grande del Norte National Monument

The Rio Pueblo (lower left in the photo) flows into the Rio Grande at the center in the Rio Grande del Norte National Monument. The National Monument was proclaimed by President Obama on March 25, 2013. It extends along the Rio Grande from the Colorado border to Pilar, New Mexico, about 12 miles south of Taos. It encompasses 240,000 acres. The highest point in the monument is Ute Mountain with an elevation of 10,093 feet, while the river itself is 565 feet below the Rio Grande Gorge Bridge west of Taos.

The Rio Grande is America's fifth longest river. It is 1,800 miles long, with its source at Stony Pass near Silverton, Colorado and its mouth at the Gulf of Mexico. In the National Monument it flows through a rift valley which was formed about 30 million years ago by shifting earth plates which caused faults or cracks in the earth's crust. The Rio Grande Rift is thus a long sliver of earth's crust that dropped down between two lines of faults. The river itself did not create the rift. It flows through the natural passageway of the rift, and over millions of years has deepened the rift through its erosive forces.

With great support from the citizens of northern New Mexico, the Rio Grande del Norte National Monument was created to protect four key "objects of value." First, it protects the area's unique geology with the rift valley and the volcanic cones rising to the west of the river. Second, it safeguards cultural and historic resources in the area such as petroglyphs (images carved into the gorge's dark basalt cliffs) and historic Native American artifacts such as pottery which are scattered across the forested slopes of the volcanic cones. Third, it protects the ecological diversity of the area seen in the cottonwood and willow trees along the river, sagebrush on the plains, piñon pines on the volcanic cones, and spruce, aspen and Douglas fir trees on the higher slopes. Finally, it protects the diverse wildlife of the area which includes birds, fish, river otters, elk, deer, antelope and bighorn sheep.

Recreation is also a very important aspect of the National Monument with hiking trails, fishing, camping, and rafting. There is a visitor center in Pilar, and established campgrounds just west of Pilar, and at Wild Rivers north of Questa.

RIO GRANDE GORGE BRIDGE
TWELVE MILES WEST OF TAOS ON U.S. 64

Ridiculed as "the bridge to nowhere," the Gorge Bridge was opened on September 10, 1965. Its very purpose was to open northern New Mexico to tourists and development. Prior to the Gorge Bridge, there were only two ways to cross the river by primitive gravel roads over the John Dunn Bridge west of Arroyo Hondo, and the Taos Junction Bridge northwest of Pilar. Other crossings were farther north in Colorado.

In 1959 a group of civic leaders formed the U.S. 64 Association to advocate extending U.S. Highway 64 from Taos west across northern New Mexico. In 1960 a cost estimate for the bridge came in at $1.5 million, which was deemed too expensive. In 1962, New Mexico governor Jack Campbell pushed for the construction of the Gorge Bridge to create an east-west highway across northern New Mexico. Groundbreaking for the bridge began on July 11, 1963. The first step in construction was to create a tramway across the Gorge which could ferry men and materials from one side to the other.

The bridge, as constructed, is a three span continuous deck truss structure. It required 2,000 tons of steel and 60 tons of bolts. The two supporting piers are 105 feet tall, with 15 feet below ground to bedrock, which is the dark black basalt (lava) rock seen on the sides of the gorge. No one died in the constructions of the bridge, but there were numerous minor injuries caused mainly by falling objects such as bolts, nuts, and pins. The bridge is designed to move- it would collapse if it was completely rigid. It is about 2,000 feet long and 565 feet above the river.

The Gorge Bridge accomplished its goal of linking the small communities of northern New Mexico and increasing visitation to the area. It is one of the main tourist attractions in the Taos area. Visitors can park in designated areas and walk across the sidewalks of the bridge from one side to the other, feeling the bridge sway as cars pass on the pavement. A recent addition is the help-line telephones which have been installed along the sidewalks. Unfortunately the bridge attracts suicide victims, and approximately 45 people have died leaping over the edge since 1965.

Founded in 1955, Taos Ski Valley is the brainchild of Ernie Blake, its original owner, who cut the first trails and put in the first lift. Ernest Hermann Bloch was born in Frankfurt, Germany in 1913, to a Swiss mother and a German father. When he joined the U.S. Army in 1943, the Army changed his name to "Blake" to remove the implications of the Jewish name "Bloch." But that's getting ahead of the story. Ernie took his mother's Swiss citizenship and went to school in Switzerland, where skiing was part of the curriculum. He served in the Swiss air force from 1933-1935. His family emigrated to New York City in 1938 when the political situation in Germany was becoming dicey.

In the U.S.A., Ernie got involved in ski racing in the Rocky Mountains, and he met many of the pioneers of the U.S. ski industry. He began dreaming of owning his own ski area, but World War II intervened. Ernie desperately wanted to join the 10th Mountain Division which trained skiers for combat in the European mountains. However, the Army initially thought he was a German spy, and would not accept him. Finally, in 1943 the Army accepted him, changed his name to Blake, and conferred U.S. citizenship upon him. Ernie was placed in Military Intelligence because of his command of French, German and Italian. Eventually he was sent to England, where he spent the rest of the war interrogating captured German officers.

After the war, Blake came home and he and his wife Rhoda settled in New Mexico, where Ernie became general manager of Santa Fe Ski Basin. Blake then began his search for his own ski area, flying his Cessna 170 plane over the Rocky Mountains from Santa Fe to Glenwood Springs, Colorado searching for the perfect spot. He found it in Twining Canyon, some seventeen miles north of Taos. Twining was an old mining camp up the Rio Hondo at the base of Wheeler Peak, New Mexico's highest peak. It generally received over 300 inches of snow per year, and the incredibly steep slopes reminded Blake of his Swiss skiing days. Thus the Bavarian-type ski village which was later developed at the base of the ski area.

Ernie Blake died in 1989, and his ashes were scattered by plane over his mountain. The Blake family held on to Taos Ski Valley until late 2013, when they sold it to billionaire hedge-fund manager Louis Bacon. Bacon, a devoted conservationist, has pledged to honor the heritage of Taos Ski Valley, while putting in new developments such as the Blake Hotel (opened in 2017) to attract more visitors to the ski area.

La Hacienda De Los Martinez
Ranchitos Road (two miles southwest of Taos Plaza)

In 1804 Don Antonio Severino Martinez moved his family from Abiquiu to this ranch on the Rio Pueblo, just outside of Taos. With his wife Maria and their six children, they expanded the original four-room building into the massive adobe fortress containing 21 rooms seen on the following page. Their home was built as a fort to provide protection from raiding Comanche and Apache Indians. There are no windows along the walls, and loopholes for guns can be seen along the top above the canales, where defenders could fire down into attackers. The only entrances were a single door, and a large door for wagons and livestock. The ladder seen in the photograph is a late addition, and would not have been there during the time of the Indian raids.

Inside the fortress were two open plazas, which provided the only daylight for the occupants. The Martinez family used the front plaza, and their servants and workers used the rear plaza, which also housed the livestock. The preserved hacienda provides a glimpse of Spanish colonial life in New Mexico. The building is operated as a museum today, under the auspices of Taos Historic Museums.

La Hacienda de los Martinez was a very important trading center in the 1800s in northern New Mexico. It was at the northern end of El Camino Real (the Royal Highway) which ran from Mexico City to Santa Fe and Taos. The Martinez family and their laborers produced animal skins, jerked meat, grain, wool and piñon nuts, which they hauled south by oxcart and mule to be traded in Chihuahua, Mexico for sugar, chocolate, iron tools, shoes, ink and paper. Don Martinez became wealthy on this trade, and was a prominent early Hispanic citizen of Taos, serving as mayor.

Antonio Jose Martinez, the Don's oldest son, was born in Abiquiu in January, 1793, so he was eleven years old when the family moved to Taos. He received a Catholic education in Durango, Mexico, and was ordained as a priest. Padre Martinez became parish priest of Our Lady of Guadalupe Church in Taos in 1826. He was heavily involved in Taos affairs, bringing in the first printing press, and printing the first newspaper and first book in New Mexico. He also established the first coeducational school in Taos. Padre Martinez' worldly ways involved him in a bitter feud with Archbishop Lamy of Santa Fe, which is detailed in Willa Cather's fictional book *Death Comes For the Archbishop*. Today, there is a life-size statue of Padre Martinez on Taos Plaza.

St. Francis of Assisi Church
Ranchos de Taos Plaza

The village of Ranchos de Taos adjoins the town of Taos on its southern border. Just south of the stoplight in Ranchos and beyond the post office, a left turn will bring the traveler to the Ranchos de Taos Plaza, with its famous St. Francis of Assisi Church. Ranchos de Taos is located on the Cristobal de la Serna land grant, which was awarded to Captain Cristobal de la Serna by the Spanish crown in April, 1710 for his service at Taos Pueblo. Ranchers began settling on the grant in the 1730s, and by 1760 a village had arisen in Ranchos de Taos.

Unfortunately, Ranchos de Taos immediately came under severe attacks by Comanche warriors, and residents fled for their lives to Taos Pueblo, where they stayed until 1779. When the attacks finally decreased, the governor of New Mexico allowed Ranchos residents to return there with the condition that they build their homes in a square plaza surrounded by a high wall for defensive purposes.

By 1812, Ranchos de Taos had grown considerably, and residents applied for a license with the Archdiocese of Durango, Mexico for a license to build their own church so that they would not have to travel to Taos to worship at Our Lady of Guadalupe Church or to San Geronimo Church at Taos Pueblo. The license was granted in September of 1813, and construction of the church began immediately. It was a massive undertaking for the residents of Ranchos. One hundred thousand hand-formed adobe bricks had to be made. Thirty-two vigas (roof logs) each at least 32 feet long had to be cut from the mountain forest to support the roof in the nave and 28 vigas 25 feet long were cut for the transept. The church was finished in 1815, with a total length of 120 feet, and ten foot wide buttresses at the back of the church (seen in the photograph).

The adobe bricks of the exterior walls of the church have to be "re-mudded" nearly every year. Rain and snow degrade the mud covering the bricks, and if the exterior walls are not re-mudded, the adobe bricks begin to disintegrate. Re-mudding is a process known as the "enjarre" when all church members come together for about two weeks in the summer to re-mud the church. Traditionally, women (known as "enjarradoras") did the re-mudding, but in modern times the task has fallen to men and women of the church and community. The church has become well-known internationally from photographs by Ansel Adams, and paintings by Georgia O'Keeffe and other artists.

TAOS MORADA
PENITENTE ROAD

Moradas are found in villages throughout northern New Mexico. They are meeting houses of Los Hermanos Penitentes (the Penitent Brotherhood). In the far-flung Spanish empire of New Mexico there were never enough Catholic priests to serve all the scattered villages. In the absence of priests the Penitentes were a group of laymen who provided needed services for Catholic parishioners such as conducting prayer services, saying the rosary, tending the sick, and burying the dead.

The Penitentes carried on a tradition of self-flagellation during Holy Week before Easter, a practice which had developed in the late Middle Ages in Europe. The Brothers whipped themselves with cactus thorn whips, and carried a heavy wooden cross to a secluded high hill where the crucifixion of Christ was re-enacted. They tied one of their brothers to the cross, and due to the extreme stress of carrying the cross and bearing the torture, some Penitentes did actually die on the cross. Due to the brutality of this practice, Archbishop Lamy of Santa Fe vigorously opposed the Brotherhood in the 1850s. In 1889 the Vatican banned the Brotherhood entirely. The Brotherhood then became even more secretive, and carried on their practices. In 1947 Archbishop Edwin Byrnes of Santa Fe finally recognized the Brotherhood once more on the condition that they stop the practice of self-flagellation.

Along the High Road to Taos, moradas can be found in many of the villages. In my book (*High Road To Taos*) there are photographs of moradas in Truchas, Las Trampas, and Vadito. There are also two moradas in Talpa, just south of Taos. In Taos visitors can find the morada by turning off Kit Carson Road north to Las Cruces Road, and then left on Penitente Road.

The Taos morada was constructed in about 1860. It is a typical adobe structure with a flat roof and "canales" for draining water off the roof. There are two windows and three buttresses on the west side. On the roof there is a bell tower with a white cross at the top. The morada has two rooms, the largest of which is a chapel with an altar for prayer services. The smaller room is a meeting room for discussions. Visitors are never allowed in the morada, and are asked to be respectful when visiting the grounds.

GOVERNOR BENT HOUSE AND MUSEUM
117 BENT STREET

Tucked just behind some shops on the north side of Bent Street, the visitor will see a sign for the Governor Bent House and Museum. This was the residence of Charles Bent and his family. Bent was an American trader married to Mexican citizen Maria Jaramillo. Bent and his brother George and their partner Ceran St. Vrain, established several trading posts along the Santa Fe Trail including Adobe Walls in the Texas panhandle, Bent's Fort in southeastern Colorado, Santa Fe and Taos. The trade was quite lucrative as manufactured goods were brought west from Missouri, and buffalo hides and beaver skins were shipped back east. The Bent wagon trains hauled these goods back and forth across the frontier.

In the war with Mexico in 1846, American troops invaded and conquered Santa Fe without firing a shot. The new American territory of New Mexico then needed a governor, and loyal American citizen Charles Bent of Taos was appointed. Bent went to Santa Fe to tend to the government. On January 14, 1847 Bent traveled back to Taos with the intention of bringing his wife and children to Santa Fe. He encountered angry mobs in Taos consisting of Taos Pueblo Indians and Mexican citizens who wanted no part of the American takeover. On January 19, 1847 the mobs attacked the home of Charles Bent who was inside with his wife, children, and his wife's sister Josefa Carson who was the wife of Kit Carson. Bent held off the intruders long enough so that the women and children could escape through a hole they dug in the adobe wall into the adjoining home. The mob broke into the home and killed and scalped Charles Bent. Several more Americans were killed in the melee.

This "Taos Revolt" was quelled when Colonel Sterling Price of the U.S. Army marched north from Santa Fe with 335 soldiers through deep snow over the mountains to Taos. With information that the insurgents were taking shelter in the church at Taos Pueblo, the Army bombarded the church, destroying it and killing many innocent civilians. Alleged perpetrators of the Revolt were rounded up and brought to trial in Taos. They were found guilty and hanged in Taos Plaza. The trial and its results were probably a foregone conclusion since the judge was Charles Beaubien who was the father of one of the victims of the Revolt, and the jury foreman was George Bent, brother of murdered Governor Charles Bent.

Kit Carson Home and Museum
113 Kit Carson Road

As Taos historian Bob Romero has noted, "the legacy of Kit Carson as a historical figure is an enigma as he is viewed as both a hero and a villain depending on the community and perspective... From the Native American perspective he is certainly not a hero, but from the Anglo American perspective he 'led the way' and helped open the West for American settlement and expansion." During his lifetime Carson was a fur trapper, explorer and guide, Indian agent, U.S. Army officer, and Indian fighter.

Christopher "Kit" Carson was born on December 24, 1809 in Kentucky, but his family soon moved to Missouri. From there Carson left his family at age 17 to venture west on the Santa Fe Trail, eventually ending up in Taos. In Taos he was heavily involved in beaver trapping and the fur trade. When the fur trade died out about 1840, his mountain man travel experience served him well as he became a guide for John C. Fremont's 1842 expedition to California. In 1846 he again served as a California guide, this time for Colonel Stephen Watts Kearney, who had just completed the American conquest of New Mexico. In between, Carson married his third wife, Josefa Jaramillo, in Taos, and purchased a four-room adobe home in 1843, which is now the museum. The Carsons had eight children, and Josefa died in 1868 during the birth of their eighth child.

Kit Carson served as an Indian agent for the U.S. Government from 1854–1861. He was an agent for the Taos Pueblo, Jicarilla Apache, and Ute tribes. He used a room in his Taos home as an office where he met with many of the Indian leaders. In 1861 he became an officer in the U.S. Army, and in 1862 he fought in battles driving the Confederate Army out of New Mexico. In 1863 he helped subdue the Mescalero Apaches in New Mexico, and in 1864 the Comanche and Navajo tribes. Under the orders of his superior officer, he pursued a "scorched earth" policy where he burned the Indians' agricultural fields, gardens and fruit trees. Facing starvation, the Indians surrendered.

After subduing the Navajo in Canyon de Chelly, Arizona, Carson (again acting under orders), forced the Navajo tribe to endure the infamous "Long Walk" where the army marched them hundreds of miles south to a reservation in eastern New Mexico. Hundreds of Navajo died on the journey. After the Indian wars, Carson tried ranching at Boggsville, Colorado. He died on May 23, 1868, one month after Josefa's death. They are both buried in Kit Carson Cemetery in Taos.

Long John Dunn House and Bridge
House—124 Bent Street
Bridge—West of Arroyo Hondo

"Long" John Dunn was one of the most colorful early Anglo characters of Taos, arriving from Texas in 1889 when he was 32, and dying in Taos in 1953. He earned the nickname "Long" because of his height (6' 4") and slim build. "Long" also described his life of 96 years. As his biographer Max Evans wrote, "He was top-notch in everything he did. John was one of the best gunfighters, gamblers, bronc riders, ropers, stagecoach drivers, trail-herd drivers, saloonkeepers, outlaws and, ironically, hardheaded businessmen."

Long John Dunn arrived in Taos in 1889 after killing his brother-in-law in a fight in Texas. Dunn was sentenced to life in prison, but he escaped while working on a chain gang, and made his way to Mexico. Eventually he drifted north to Taos. In Taos he established saloons, hotels and gambling joints. From his trail-driving days in Texas he was an accomplished horseman and stage driver. He established a thriving stagecoach business in Taos, picking up passengers from the rail line some 25 miles west of Taos. He built a wooden bridge across the Rio Grande west of Arroyo Hondo, and charged his stage passengers for the ride as well as a toll for crossing the bridge. It was quite a lucrative business.

The railroad never came in to Taos. The Denver and Rio Grande Railroad expanded south from Antonito, Colorado all the way south to Santa Fe in 1881. This was known as the "Chili Line" because of the "ristras" (strings of chili peppers) hanging outside the homes along the line. The train stopped at Servilleta, ten miles south of Tres Piedras. Here John Dunn met the train with his stagecoach and transported passengers on the long bumpy ride east across the plateau, down the switchbacks to the Rio Grande, across the bridge he built, up the switchbacks to Arroyo Hondo, and then south to Taos. A pregnant female passenger once asked Long John if the bumpy ride would affect her condition, and he replied "I don't know ma'am, I've never been in your condition."

Long John Dunn built a ten-room adobe house on Bent Street in Taos, which still stands today. Travelers on Bent Street can visit the retail shops which inhabit the house. The steel truss bridge seen in the photograph replaced John's wooden bridge in the early 1900s, but it is still known as the John Dunn Bridge. There is a sign directing travelers to its location off of New Mexico Highway 522 northwest of Taos.

HISTORIC TAOS INN
125 PASEO DEL PUEBLO NORTE

This famous inn dates back to the late 1800s when the building was purchased in 1891 by Dr. Thomas Paul Martin, the first and only physician in Taos at the time. Doc Martin bought one of the largest homes in Taos to serve as his office, surgery and home. He was a true "horse and buggy" doctor, making house calls throughout the area. He continued his service for over forty years, later trading in his buggy for an automobile. Many of Doc's patients could not pay him for his services, so he accepted "in-kind" items such as a bag of potatoes, a chicken, or a side of venison.

In the dining room of today's inn is a glass alcove in the southwest corner which served as Doc's baby delivery room and surgery because of the excellent natural light there. Doc's sister Rose was married to artist Bert Phillips, and she recalled that it was in this room that her husband and Ernest Blumenschein came up with the idea of the Taos Society of Artists. Diners in this room today are feasting in a truly historic spot. It was also in Doc Martin's home that the very first meeting of the Taos Society of Artists occurred on July 15, 1915.

After Doc's death in 1936, his wife Helen converted the home and office into an inn which she named the Hotel Martin. In 1948 she sold the hotel to Harold and Hilda Street who renamed it the Taos Inn, and that has remained its name through several owners up to the present time.

The Taos Inn is one of the favorite gathering places of Taosenos and visitors alike. Its two-story high lobby with a glass cupola on top houses an enormous Christmas tree for the holidays. To the south of the lobby is the famous Adobe Bar which hosts nightly musical entertainment. And to the north of the lobby is Doc Martin's Restaurant, serving delicious southwest cuisine in Doc Martin's old office area. Local artists are often invited to display their works on the walls of the lobby and restaurant.

Taos Society of Artists: Ernest Blumenschein Home and Museum
222 Ledoux Street

In the 1890s artists from America's east coast discovered Taos and its fantastic light, colors, scenery and Pueblo Indians. In 1893 artist Joseph Henry Sharp ventured in to Taos after taking the train to Santa Fe. On assignment for *Harper's Weekly* magazine, he sketched the incredible scenery and Taos Pueblo which captivated him. Two years later, while studying at the Academie Julian in Paris, Sharp met two young American artists also studying there- Ernest Blumenschein and Bert Geer Phillips. Sharp told them about Taos, and enchanted them with stories about the place.

Back in the United States, Blumenschein and Phillips decided to take Sharp's advice and visit Taos. They started from Denver in a wagon in September, 1898, hoping to go all the way to Mexico, sketching and painting along the way. About 20 miles north of Taos a wheel on the wagon broke. Having no way to repair the wheel, it had to be taken to a blacksmith in Taos. They flipped a coin to see who would take the wheel to Taos, and Blumenschein lost. He loaded the wheel onto his horse, and proceeded to Taos. With the wheel repaired, Blumenschein returned to Phillips and they went on to Taos together. They both were captivated by the place and immediately began painting. Phillips stayed in Taos permanently, while Blumenschein returned to New York and then Paris.

Phillips soon wrote to Blumenschein, "For heaven's sake, tell people what we have found. Send some artists out here. There's a lifetime of work for 20 men." And so the artists came to Taos. In July, 1915, Blumenschein, Phillips and their old friend Sharp (who had since moved to Taos) formed the Taos Society of Artists along with three other men: Oscar Berninghaus, E. Irving Couse, and W. Herbert "Buck" Dunton. The purpose of the society was to show their work in galleries back east and find buyers for their art. They were very successful in their efforts.

Blumenschein married American artist Mary Greene in Paris in 1905, and they moved permanently to Taos in 1919. They bought a four-room home on Ledoux Street from Buck Dunton. When rooms adjacent to the home became unoccupied, they were added to the home. The museum complex now consists of ten rooms, and Dunton's old studio is on the grounds of the property.

Taos Society of Artists: Bert Geer Phillips Home and Studio
136 Paseo del Pueblo Norte

Bert Phillips was the very embodiment of a romanticist. Growing up in Hudson, New York where he was born in 1868, he read James Fenimore Cooper's Leatherstocking Tales and became fascinated with Indians. Another of his heroes was Kit Carson, whom he read about in fanciful dime novels. It was no wonder that Phillips fell in love with Taos when he stumbled upon it in 1898 with Ernest Blumenschein. After all, this was the home of Kit Carson and the Taos Pueblo Indians.

Phillips first studio in Taos was located next to the old Governor Bent home. A few years later he moved to a studio and home at the corner of Paseo del Pueblo Norte and Martyrs Lane (named after the martyrs of the 1847 Taos revolt). This studio had a huge north-facing skylight window, which can still be seen in the building today. In 1899 Phillips married Rose Martin, the sister of Doc Martin, Taos' first physician, and they later had two children.

In 1907 Phillips was having trouble with his vision, perhaps as a result of eye strain from painting in dark smoky rooms. He decided he had to give up painting for a while, and he became a forest ranger for the Taos Forest Reserve. When the Taos Reserve was combined with the Jemez Reserve in 1908, Phillips proposed the name of Kit Carson National Forest, in honor of his boyhood hero. The name was enthusiastically adopted. By 1909, Phillips eyesight had improved and he returned to painting.

Bert Phillips and Ernest Blumenschein were heavily involved in persuading more artists to move to Taos, and together they conceived the idea of the Taos Society of Artists to promote and sell their work. Phillips was always eager to find accommodations for new artists coming to Taos. The Society soon expanded from its original six members to a total of ten, including new arrivals Victor Higgins, Walter Ufer, E. Martin Hennings, and Kenneth Adams. Later, two final members were added: Julius Rolshoven and Catharine Critcher, the Society's only female member.

Bert Phillips former home and studio are inhabited today by a gallery and gift shop and are open to visitors during business hours. Phillips painted Taos scenes and Pueblo Indians from the time he moved here in 1898 until his death in June, 1956.

Taos Society of Artists: Couse/Sharp Historic Site
146 Kit Carson Road

This historic site consisting of several buildings, was the home of Eanger Irving Couse and the home and studios of Joseph Henry Sharp. Sharp first purchased a home on Kit Carson Road in 1908, and he purchased the adjacent Luna Chapel for his studio in 1909. Entering the historic site, the Luna Chapel is the shaded building on the right in the photograph, and the Couse home is straight ahead. The Luna Chapel was built in the 1830s by Juan de Luna as a chapel for his family. When Sharp purchased it in 1909, he knocked out a large portion of wall on the north side for a window for his studio. However, finding the chapel still too dark for his work, he built a new studio in 1915 out of a house that existed behind his house. This studio has been restored by the Couse Foundation and was opened to the public in 2017.

Joseph Henry Sharp was born in Bridgeport, Ohio in 1859. He studied at the Cincinnati Art Academy, and then at the Academie Julian in Paris. His first trip to the American west was in 1883, and he was captivated by the landscape and the Indians. In 1893 he made his first trip to Taos, and it was this adventure that he told to Ernest Blumenschein and Bert Phillips in Paris, which piqued their interest and their subsequent "broken wheel" trip to Taos in 1898. Sharp moved to Crow Agency, Montana in 1902 to paint the Plains Indians. By 1908 he was back in Taos, where he found the Taos Pueblo Indians to be willing models for his paintings.

Eanger Irving Couse was born in Saginaw, Michigan on September 3, 1866. He enrolled in the Art Institute of Chicago in 1883, and in 1886 he went to study at the Academie Julian in Paris. There he studied under famous artist William Bouguereau, whose techniques influenced him throughout his life. He married American artist Virginia Walker in Paris in 1889, and they moved to Washington in 1896 near the home of Virginia's family. There, Couse painted portraits of Northwest Coast Indians, but by 1902 was lacking models for his work. His old friend from Paris, Ernest Blumenschein, suggested that Couse move on to Taos, which he did in 1902. The Couse's eventually purchased a home on Kit Carson Road adjacent to Sharp's home in 1909.

Couse and Sharp were founding members of the Taos Society of Artists in 1915, and Couse was elected its first president. Today, the Couse/Sharp Historic Site consists of the Couse home, the Luna Chapel, Sharp's restored studio behind the Couse home, and Sharpe's home (the former Mission Gallery) which will be restored and serve as the Archive Center for the site.

Taos Society of Artists: Victor Higgins Home and Studio
122D Kit Carson Road

Victor Higgins was born on June 28, 1884 in Shelbyville, Indiana. At the age of 15 he left home to study art at the Art Institute of Chicago and the Chicago Academy of Fine Art. He remained in Chicago for ten years, before leaving for Europe in 1911, where he studied in England, Paris and Munich. In Munich he met E. Martin Hennings and Walter Ufer, both future members of the Taos Society of Artists.

Higgins returned to Chicago in 1913, and in 1914 long-time Chicago mayor and art patron Carter Harrison Jr. commissioned Higgins to do a landscape painting of Taos. Taos artists were well known in Chicago due to their numerous art shows there. Harrison's familiarity with Higgins work prompted him to pay all of Higgins expenses to travel to Taos and paint there. Thus Higgins arrived in Taos in 1914, and became a permanent resident in 1915. Both Victor Higgins and Walter Ufer were invited to join the Taos Society of Artists in 1917.

Higgins married Sara Parsons, daughter of Santa Fe painter Sheldon Parsons, in 1919. He was 35 and she was 18. This disparity in their ages probably had a lot to do with their divorce five years later. They lived at a home on Mabel Dodge Luhan's property, and both became good friends with Mabel. The home on Kit Carson Road was a later home and studio for Victor Higgins. In 1946, Higgins returned to the "Saint Theresa House" on Mabel's property where he lived until his death in 1949.

The property on Kit Carson Road became the home of the famous Taos Book Shop in the 1950s. Founded by Claire Morrill and Genevieve Janssen in 1947, the shop later moved from Taos Plaza to Kit Carson Road. The Taos Book Shop lasted under various owners until the 1990s. Today the building is home to Robert Parsons Gallery of the West. If visitors peek into the office in the gallery, they can see the old "Taos Book Shop" sign still hanging there.

Mabel Dodge Luhan House
240 Morada Lane

Mabel Ganson was born on February 26, 1879 to wealthy socialite parents in Buffalo, New York. Her chaotic life which followed, featured numerous love affairs (both men and women), marriages, divorces, and homes from New York, to Italy to Taos, New Mexico. She married her first husband, Karl Evans, in Buffalo in 1900. This marriage produced a son, John, but it ended tragically in 1902 when Karl was killed by a friend in a hunting accident. Mabel soon left on a sea voyage to Europe and met Boston architect Edwin Dodge, whom she married in 1904. They had a villa in Florence, Italy until 1912, where they entertained American artists and writers visiting Europe. During her time in Italy, Mabel had numerous affairs and eventually divorced Dodge, returning to New York.

Mabel took an apartment in Greenwich Village in New York City, and soon began entertaining "movers and shakers" there. She met painter/sculptor Maurice Sterne and married him in 1916. Sterne went to New Mexico in 1917, and soon urged Mabel to join him. She immediately fell in love with Taos and bought a four-room adobe house in 1918 for $1,500. The house adjoined Taos Pueblo land, and while teaching some Taos Pueblo women how to knit, she met Tony Luhan, a Taos Pueblo Indian who became her fourth husband in 1923. Mabel and Tony began expanding the original house, and Tony supervised a crew of Taos Pueblo Indians who enlarged the home to the 22 rooms present there today.

Such a large home in Taos enabled Mabel to entertain artists, photographers, and writers from around the country. Artists could come to Taos and stay at Mabel's for relaxation and inspiration. Visitors included photographer Ansel Adams; artists Georgia O'Keefe, Edward Hopper, and Lady Dorothy Brett; writers Willa Cather, D.H. Lawrence, Frank Waters, and Aldous Huxley; psychologist Carl Jung; and John Collier, who as U.S. Commissioner of Indian Affairs from 1933 to 1945, was deeply involved in protecting the rights of Taos Pueblo Indians.

Besides attracting artists to Taos, Mabel was instrumental in purchasing and preserving art works from the Taos Indians. She became a strong proponent of native art. So despite her questionable sexual mores, Mabel Evans Dodge Sterne Luhan is rightfully remembered as helping to establish Taos as an artist's colony and retreat for artists from around the country. Mabel died on August 13, 1962 and is buried in Kit Carson cemetery. Tony Luhan died soon after Mabel, and is buried in the Taos Pueblo cemetery. Today the Mabel Dodge Luhan House continues to be a retreat center, offering classes, programs and relaxation for people drawn to Taos by its natural beauty and cultural diversity.

Nicolai Fechin House/Taos Art Museum
227 Paseo del Pueblo Norte

Nicolai Fechin was born in Kazan, Russia in 1881. He studied art at the Imperial Art Academy in Petrograd for seven years, and became an art teacher in Russia. In 1913 he married Alexandra Belkovitch. While teaching, Fechin began submitting his art work to the Chicago Art Institute and the Carnegie Institute in Pittsburgh. His work was well received, so the Fechins along with daughter Eya, moved to New York City in 1923. They lived there for four years and Fechin became one of the leading portrait painters in the city.

In the summer of 1926, the Fechins visited Taos at the suggestion of British portrait painter John Young-Hunter. They loved the area, and moved to Taos in 1927, purchasing an adobe home on Paseo. Fechin completely redesigned and rebuilt the home, adding his wood carving skills to the furniture, corbels, grand staircase, and just about every other piece of wood in the house. He had a studio back of the house (today housing the museum gift shop) which had a high ceiling with a huge north-facing glass window. Fechin painted in the early morning hours when the light was best in his studio, and at other times of the day worked on his wood carving and sculpture.

Unfortunately, Nicolai and Alexandra divorced in 1933. Alexandra continued to live in the home until her death in 1983. Nicolai moved to California where he had a studio in Santa Monica. He died in California in 1955. After Alexandra's death, daughter Eya took over care of the Fechin home in Taos. She established the Fechin Institute and opened a museum in the home. Eya died in November, 2002, and the Taos Art Museum made plans to move into the home.

The Taos Art Museum was founded in 1994 to preserve the works of early 20th century Taos artists. In late 2002, the Museum moved into the Fechin home, and opened there in July 2003. The Museum displays works from its collection of paintings by the Taos Society of Artists as well as paintings by Fechin. The house itself is a wonderful work of art, and visitors will enjoy seeing its interior, the fabulous paintings hung on the walls, and the gift shop in the studio which has a great selection of books about Taos artists.

HISTORIC TAOS COUNTY COURTHOUSE
NORTH SIDE, TAOS PLAZA

Constructed in 1932, the Taos County Courthouse located on the Plaza, was the third courthouse to serve the county. Taos County was created by the New Mexico Territorial Legislature in 1852. The first courthouse served for 28 years until it was replaced by a courthouse on the plaza in 1880 in today's location. This second courthouse was destroyed by fire in 1932. Louis Hesselden of Albuquerque was the architect for this third courthouse which was completed in late 1932.

In 1968 plans were developed for a new modern courthouse and jail facility to replace the cramped old courthouse on the Plaza. The new facility was completed in 1970 on Paseo del Pueblo Sur, about a mile south of Taos Plaza. The historic courthouse on the Plaza was then transformed into offices, galleries and shops, much like it is today. As of this writing though, change is in the air, with restoration planned for the building including a museum of the Taos County Historical Society on the second floor where the old courthouse chambers were previously located.

Visitors are welcome at the historic courthouse, and on the first floor they can see the old jail cells. Here, scenes for the movie Easy Rider were shot in 1969. Starring Peter Fonda, Dennis Hopper, and Jack Nicholson, the film is a counterculture classic.

The flagpole on Taos Plaza has an interesting history also. In 1861 Confederate soldiers from Texas began invading New Mexico, with hopes of taking the state and moving on to California. Confederate sympathizers in Taos hoisted a Confederate flag in Taos Plaza. Kit Carson, as a Union soldier, was disgusted with this act. Carson, Ceran St. Vrain and several other men tore down the Confederate flag, and replaced it with the Union flag. They then guarded the flagpole day and night to keep the Confederate sympathizers away. In March, 1862 the Confederate Army was defeated at the Battle of Glorieta Pass (just southeast of Santa Fe) by Union soldiers supplemented by soldiers from Fort Garland, Colorado, just north of the New Mexico border. The Confederate Army retreated to Texas, never to return. In a twist of fate, Kit Carson became the commandant of Fort Garland in 1866.

Historic Courthouse Fresco Murals

On the second floor of the Historic Taos County Courthouse on Taos Plaza, are ten colorful fresco murals created in 1934 by Taos artists Emil Bisttram, Ward Lockwood, Bert Phillips, and Victor Higgins. Phillips and Higgins had been members of the Taos Society of Artists which disbanded in 1927. Artists across America were severely impacted by the Great Depression when buyers for their work vanished overnight. To aid the "starving artists," the Public Works Art Project of President Franklin Roosevelt's Works Progress Administration, commissioned artists across the country to paint murals in public buildings. In Taos, the four artists were commissioned for the courthouse murals.

Heading the mural project was Santa Fe artist Gustav Baumann, well-known for his colorful wood-block prints. Baumann suggested that the murals depict historic scenes, but the artists had another theme in mind based on the courthouse location. They suggested "justice" as the theme, and Baumann agreed with them. They created dramatic and vivid scenes of social realism, with each work titled in English and Spanish. The centerpiece and largest mural was Victor Higgins' "Moses The Lawgiver" depicting Moses with the Ten Commandments (next page). This was Higgins only mural, as the other artists painted three murals each, for a total of ten.

The frescoes were finished in three months by the end of March, 1934. Frescoes are created by painting tempera pigment and distilled water on the wall surface which has been prepared with several layers of lime plaster. The frescoes were restored in 1994 by Frederico Vigil, who added one of his own to the wall at the rear of the room.

The frescoes are located in what was originally the courtroom on the second floor. They are usually available for viewing by the public when the Courthouse is unlocked during the day.

For images of these frescoes, refer to the book, *A More Abundant Life* by Jacqueline Hoefer in the bibliography.

MOSES·THE·LAW·GIVER   MOISES·EL·LEGISLADOR

Harwood Museum of Art
238 Ledoux Street

When Burt (1857–1922) and wife Elizabeth (1867–1938) Harwood moved to Taos in 1916, they left their home in France where Burt was an artist and photographer. Burt suffered from tuberculosis, and perhaps the dry desert air of Taos is what attracted him here. The Harwoods purchased a property on Ledoux Street which contained several adobe buildings. Over the next two years Burt redesigned, remodeled and added to the complex, creating "El Pueblito" or the "little village" whose design was strongly influenced by Taos Pueblo.

The complex soon became known in Taos as simply "The Harwood." Art exhibitions were held there as early as 1924, and the tradition continues to this day. In 1926, Elizabeth started loaning out books from her private collection because Taos had no public library at the time. Mabel Dodge Luhan supported the nascent Harwood library by donating her own books and money. The Taos library remained at the Harwood until 1996, when the town finally opened its own public library in a building constructed just west of Town Hall.

In 1923, a year after Burt's death, Elizabeth formed the Harwood Foundation as a private nonprofit organization. In 1935 Elizabeth transferred ownership of the property to the University of New Mexico, which stills owns it today. The governing board of the Harwood reports directly to the Board of Regents of the University of New Mexico. In 1937, UNM and the federal Works Projects Administration worked together to expand and renovate the Harwood. Famed southwestern architect John Gaw Meem (see "Taos First Presbyterian Church") designed the expansion including an auditorium, stage, library facility, and exhibition space.

The Harwood Museum has always emphasized its collection of Taos art, including major works by members of the Taos Society of Artists. In 2016 it mounted a major exhibition titled "Mabel Dodge Luhan and Company" which followed Mabel's career and her influence in bringing artists to Taos. Since 1945, the Harwood Museum has also represented new trends in American art, such as the work of Agnes Martin. The Museum's vision statement reflects this duality: "The Harwood Museum of Art brings Taos arts to the world and world arts to Taos."

Millicent Rogers was born in 1902 into a family of wealth. She was the granddaughter of Henry H. Rogers, one of the founders of the Standard Oil Company along with John D. Rockefeller. She grew up in New York, and was known in the press as the "Standard Oil Heiress." She became an icon on the social and fashion scene of the Roaring Twenties. She had homes in New York, Virginia, and Italy, and traveled widely throughout Europe. Her first husband was Count Ludwig Salm Von Hoogstraeten—a former Austrian calvaryman. She later married Arturo Peralta-Ramos, an Argentine sportsman, and Ronald Balcom, a Wall Street broker.

During her years on the social scene, Millicent became a designer of clothing and jewelry. When she discovered Taos in 1947 she was immediately captivated by the Native American jewelry and Spanish colonial artifacts of the area. Over just a few years she developed a massive collection of these items. Millicent contracted rheumatic fever as a child, and was sickly most of her life. The high mountain air of Taos seemed to help her health, before she died at the age of 51 in 1953. In Taos, Millicent designed and built a splendid adobe home on Ranchitos Road known as "Turtlewalk."

Millicent's collection of thousands of pieces of Southwestern art was the basis for the museum established by her son Paul Peralta-Ramos in 1956. The museum was originally housed in artist Mabel Degan's home on Ledoux Street, and then moved to the Stables Gallery on Paseo del Pueblo Norte. The Millicent Rogers Museum opened in its current location in 1968, in a large 1920s hacienda donated by Millicent's Taos friends Claude and Elizabeth Anderson.

Paul Peralta-Ramos became friends with Maria Martinez, the famed potter of San Ildefonso Pueblo. This friendship led to the donation of a large collection of pots from Maria's family to the museum. It is a highlight of the collections, along with Native American jewelry, weavings, and a large collection of Spanish colonial art. The mission of the Millicent Rogers Museum is "sharing and celebrating the arts and cultures of the Southwest." It should be on every visitor's "to-do" list when visiting Taos.

Taos First Presbyterian Church
215 Paseo Del Pueblo Norte

This church was designed by famous Southwestern architect John Gaw Meem. Meem is known for his "Santa Fe Style" or "Pueblo Revival Style" which incorporates elements from Spanish Pueblo churches and Pueblo buildings in New Mexico.

Specifications for the church were completed in 1951 with construction completed the following year. Taos banker Jack Brandenburg was a member of the church and one of the main proponents for the new church. He insisted on John Gaw Meem as the architect because Meem "knew more than anyone else about the Pueblo missions that should set the style for New Mexico churches."

The church sanctuary was planned for seating 125 people, with an additional five classrooms, meeting room and kitchen. The cost estimate was $27,773, and Dalton Montgomery was selected as builder of the church. The final completion cost turned out to be $40,218, and both Meem and Montgomery contributed to make up the difference. Church member Cameron Mactavish recalled that "Dalton wanted to tell St. Peter at the Gates that when he was on the planet earth he built the First Presbyterian Church in Taos, New Mexico."

John Gaw Meem was born in 1894 in Pelotas, Brazil of American missionary parents. Returning to the U.S., he studied engineering at Virginia Military Institute. He served in World War I and then using his bilingual skills, he worked at a bank in Rio de Janeiro. He contracted tuberculosis, and the bank sent him to Santa Fe, New Mexico to recover. He arrived in Santa Fe in 1920, and took up residence at Sunmount Sanitarium. Meem was heavily influenced by the pueblo style of architecture he saw in Santa Fe, which was prominent in the Sanitarium, the Palace of the Governors, and the recently completed New Mexico Museum of Art. Over the next 35 years his architectural firm completed plans for 650 projects (not all of which were built), most incorporating his trademark southwestern style.

GREATER WORLD EARTHSHIP COMMUNITY
1.5 MILES WEST OF RIO GRANDE GORGE BRIDGE

Heading west over U.S. Highway 64 and crossing the Rio Grande Gorge Bridge, the traveler will soon come to a group of other-worldly homes. This is the Greater World Earthship Community, consisting of some 650 acres. Of that, 347 acres is commonly owned park land. Signs point the way to the visitor center, which is an actual earthship. Here, visitors can take a self-guided tour and observe how this self-sustainable home is built.

Earthships are remarkable structures using specific building techniques to preserve the environment and generate their own power and water supplies. The basic building blocks are used automobile tires, which are stacked and rammed full with earth to form strong supporting walls. One side of the earthship is a huge glass wall which lets in sunlight, and the other side is often dug into the ground or bermed with earth to take advantage of the year-round natural earth temperature of 50 degrees. The roof is sloped so that runoff water is captured in gutters leading to the containment cistern. There are solar panels on the roof (or nearby ground) to generate electricity for the home. Some homes also have wind generators.

Each earthship is meant to be self-contained, usually off the power grid. Water from the cistern is pumped into the bathroom and kitchen for use there. Once used, the resulting gray water is captured and then pumped to the toilet or for watering the food plants growing in the front window wall. The used toilet water is flushed out to a septic tank.

Earthships are built to comply with standard building codes. Once an architect has drawn plans for the home, much of the labor can be done by the owner if so desired. Of course it takes a long time to pack all those used tires with earth. A typical earthship advertised for sale recently was a 2,100 square foot home, with two bedrooms and one bath, for $440,000. However, annual utility bills amounted to only $100.

BIBLIOGRAPHY

Archuleta, Ruben E. *Land of the Penitentes, Land of Tradition.* Pueblo West, CO: El Jefe, 2003.

Blumenschein, Helen G. *Sounds and Sights of the Taos Valley.* Santa Fe, NM: Sunstone Press, 2016.

Brett, Dorothy. *Lawrence and Brett. A Friendship.* Santa Fe: Sunstone Press, 2006. Original edition: New York: J. B. Lippincott Company, 1933.

Bunting, Bainbridge. *John Gaw Meem: Southwestern Architect.* Albuquerque, NM: University of New Mexico Press, 1988.

———. *Taos Adobes: Spanish Colonial and Territorial Architecture of the Taos Valley.* Santa Fe, NM: Fort Burgwin Research Center and Museum of New Mexico Press, 1964.

Butler, Michael. *High Road To Taos.* Charleston, SC: Arcadia Publishing, 2016.

Carson, Christopher "Kit." *Kit Carson's Own Story of His Life.* Santa Fe, NM: Sunstone Press, New Edition, 2007.

Cather, Willa. *Death Comes For the Archbishop.* New York: Alfred A. Knopf, 1927.

Chávez, Fray Angelico. *But Time and Chance, The Story of Padre Martinez of Taos, 1793–1867.* Santa Fe, NM: Sunstone Press, 1981.

———. *My Penitente Land, Reflections of Spanish New Mexico.* Santa Fe, NM: Sunstone Press, 2012.

Chronic, Halka. *Roadside Geology of New Mexico.* Missoula, MT: Mountain Press, 1987.

Cunningham, Elizabeth. *Remarkable Women of Taos.* Taos, NM: Nighthawk Press, 2013.

de Aragón, Ray John. *Padre Martinez and Bishop Lamy.* Santa Fe, NM: Sunstone Press, 2006.

———. *The Penitentes of New Mexico, Hermanos de la Luz/Brothers of the Light.* Santa Fe, NM: Sunstone Press, 2006.

Dewitt, Miriam Hapgood. *Taos: A Memory.* Albuquerque: University of New Mexico Press, 1992.

Eldredge, Charles C., et.al. *Art In New Mexico, 1900–1945: Paths To Taos and Santa Fe.* New York: Abbeville Press, 1986.

Evans, Max. *Long John Dunn of Taos.* Santa Fe, NM: Clear Light Publishers, 1993.

Farrington, William. *Los Penitentes, A Brief History.* Santa Fe, NM: Sunstone Press, 2016.

Gibson, Arrell Morgan. *The Santa Fe and Taos Art Colonies: Age of the Muses, 1900–1942.* Norman, OK; University of Oklahoma Press, 1983.

Gordon-McCutchan, R.C. *The Taos Indians and the Battle For Blue Lake.* Santa Fe, NM: Red Crane Books, 1991.

Grant, Blanche C. *When Old Trails Were New: The Story of Taos.* Santa Fe, NM: Sunstone Press, 2007 (new edition).

Hemp, Bill. *Taos Landmarks and Legends.* Los Alamos, NM: Exceptional Books, 1996.

Henderson, Russell. *Taos Incognito: Hidden Places and Spaces.* Lone Tree, CO: Blue Bench Publishing, 2015.

Hoefer, Jacqueline. *A More Abundant Life: New Deal Artists and Public Art in New Mexico.* Santa Fe, NM: Sunstone Press, 2003.

Hooker, Van Dorn and Corina A. Santistevan. *Centuries of Hands: An Architectural History of St. Francis of Assisi Church.* Santa Fe, NM: Sunstone Press, 1996.

Julyan, Robert. *The Mountains of New Mexico.* Albuquerque, NM: University of New Mexico Press, 2006.

Leavitt, Virginia Couse. *Eanger Irving Couse: Image Maker for America.* Albuquerque, NM: Albuquerque Museum, 2006.

Lehmberg, Stanford. *Churches for the Southwest: The Ecclesiastical Architecture of John Gaw Meem.* New York: Norton, 2005.

Luhan, Mabel Dodge. *Intimate Memories: Background, Volume One.* Santa Fe: Sunstone Press, 2015. Original Edition, New York: Harcourt, Brace and Company, 1933.

———. *Intimate Memories: European Experiences, Volume Two.* Santa Fe: Sunstone Press, 2015. Original Edition, Harcourt, Brace and Company, 1935

————. *Intimate Memories: Movers and Shakers, Volume Three.* Santa Fe, Sunstone Press, 2019. Original Edition, New York: Harcourt, Brace and Company, 1936.

————. *Intimate Memories: Edge of Taos Desert, An Escape to Reality, Volume Four.* Santa Fe: Sunstone Press, 2019. Original Edition, New York: Harcourt, Brace and Company, 1937.

————. *Lorenzo in Taos.* Santa Fe: Sunstone Press, 2007. Original Edition, New York: Alfred Knopf, 1932.

————. *Winter in Taos.* Santa Fe: Sunstone Press, 2007. Original Edition, New York: Harcourt, Brace and Company, 1935.

————. Lois Rudnick (editor). *Intimate Memories: The Autobiography of Mabel Dodge Luhan.* Albuquerque, NM: University of New Mexico Press, 1999.

Morrill, Claire. *A Taos Mosaic: Portrait of a New Mexico Village.* Albuquerque, NM: University of New Mexico Press, 1973.

Oxford, Andrew. *"A Fifty Year Span: How the Rio Grande Gorge Bridge Came to Be."* The Taos News, September 21, 2015.

Peters, James E. *Headless In Taos, The Dark Fated Tale of Arthur Rockford Manby.* Santa Fe, NM: Sunstone Press, 2012

Porter, Dean A., et.al. *Taos Artists and Their Patrons 1898–1950.* Notre Dame, IN: Snite Museum of Art, 1999.

Price, L. Greer (ed.). *The Geology of Northern New Mexico's Parks, Monuments and Public Lands.* Socorro, NM: New Mexico Bureau of Geology and Mineral Resources, 2010.

Reily, Nancy Hopkins. *Georgia O'Keeffe, A Private Friendship, Part I, Walking the Sun Prairie Land.* Santa Fe, NM: Sunstone Press, 2007.

————. *Georgia O'Keeffe, A Private Friendship, Part II, Walking the Abiquiu and Ghost Ranch Land.* Santa Fe, NM: Sunstone Press, 2009.

Richards, Rick. *Ski Pioneers: Ernie Blake, His Friends, and the Making of Taos Ski Valley.* Arroyo Seco, NM: Dry Gulch Publishing, 1992.

Romero, F.R. Bob. *History of Taos.* Taos, NM: Studio Karina, 2015.

Rudnick, Lois P. and Wilson-Powell, MaLin. *Mabel Dodge Luhan and Company: American Moderns and the West*. Santa Fe, NM: Museum of New Mexico Press, 2016.

Sanchez, Pedro. *Recollections of the Life of the Priest Don Antonio Jose Martinez*. Original Spanish text translated by Ray John de Aragón. Santa Fe, NM: Sunstone Press, 2006.

Santistevan, Corina A. and Julia Moore. *Taos: A Topical History*. Santa Fe, NM: Museum of New Mexico Press, 2013.

Scott, Amy. *The Taos Society of Artists*. Santa Fe, NM: Gerald Peters Gallery, 1998.

Sides, Hampton. *Blood and Thunder: The Epic Story of Kit Carson and the Conquest of the American West*. New York: Doubleday, 2006.

Simmons, Marc. *New Mexico: An Interpretive History*. Albuquerque, NM: University of New Mexico Press, 1988.

Tapia, Steve. "*Rio Grande: The Great River.*" *The Taos News*, December 31, 2015.

Tate, Bill. *The Penitentes of the Sangre De Cristos*. Santa Fe, NM: Sunstone Press, 2016.

Taylor, Anne. *Southwestern Ornamentation and Design: The Architecture of John Gaw Meem*. Santa Fe, NM: Sunstone Press, 1992.

Wallis, Michael. *En Divina Luz: The Penitente Moradas of New Mexico*. Albuquerque, NM: University of New Mexico Press, 1994.

Wetherington, Ronald K. *Ceran St. Vrain, American Frontier Entrepreneur*. Santa Fe, NM: Sunstone Press, 2012.

www.ingramcontent.com/pod-product-compliance
Lightning Source LLC
Chambersburg PA
CBHW081420090426
42738CB00017B/3429